TACTICAL PRINCIPLES

FOR THE

EMPLOYMENT OF MACHINE-GUN SECTIONS

The Naval & Military Press Ltd

Published by the
The Naval & Military Press
in association with the Royal Armouries

Unit 10 Ridgewood Industrial Park,
Uckfield, East Sussex, TN22 5QE
Tel: +44 (0) 1825 749494
Fax: +44 (0) 1825 765701

MILITARY HISTORY AT YOUR FINGERTIPS
www.naval-military-press.com

ONLINE GENEALOGY RESEARCH
www.military-genealogy.com

ONLINE MILITARY CARTOGRAPHY
www.militarymaproom.com

ROYAL
ARMOURIES

The Library & Archives Department at the
Royal Armouries Museum, Leeds, specialises
in the history and development of armour
and weapons from earliest times to the
present day. Material relating to the
development of artillery and modern
fortifications is held at the Royal
Armouries Museum, Fort Nelson.

For further information contact:
Royal Armouries Museum, Library, Armouries Drive,
Leeds, West Yorkshire LS10 1LT
Royal Armouries, Library, Fort Nelson, Down End Road, Fareham PO17 6AN

Or visit the Museum's website at
www.armouries.org.uk

TACTICAL PRINCIPLES

FOR THE

EMPLOYMENT OF MACHINE-GUN SECTIONS

(WITH ILLUSTRATIONS).

Communicated by the Austro-Hungarian School of Musketry to, and appearing in, " Streffleur's Militärische Zeitschrift," July, August, and September, 1910.

TRANSLATED BY THE GENERAL STAFF, WAR OFFICE.

LONDON:

PRINTED FOR HIS MAJESTY'S STATIONERY OFFICE,
BY HARRISON & SONS, ST. MARTIN'S LANE,
Printers in Ordinary to His Majesty.

1911.

NOTE.

These articles contain useful instruction in the methods of drawing up schemes for field practice and training of machine-gun sections, and of criticising the execution of such schemes. They are circulated to assist commanders in these respects. Their circulation is not to be considered to justify any departure from the principles and methods laid down in our official training manuals.

GENERAL STAFF,
    WAR OFFICE,
        October, 1911.

(B 1390)   Wt. w. 3657—2173   800   10/11   H & S   P 11/271

TACTICAL PRINCIPLES FOR THE EMPLOYMENT OF MACHINE-GUN SECTIONS.

INTRODUCTORY REMARKS.

Principles for the employment of machine-guns in battle are laid down in an appendix to our "Infantry Training Manual" (*Exerzierreglement für Fusstruppen*). To a large extent the application of these principles to the countless and dissimilar situations which arise in war, can be learnt theoretically and by discussion and consideration of the experiences of other officers. Far more instructive, however, are the personal experiences gained by the somewhat painful process of trial and error at manœuvres practice camps, &c. The most valuable part of such experience is that gathered at service practice under really suitable conditions.

Such conditions are, however, by no means easy to obtain. Peace considerations of time and space, danger zones, &c., often result in service practice being reduced to little more than a technical test of the fire capacity of the weapons. Very often the only approach to real service conditions lies in the fact that ball cartridge is used instead of blank.

In drawing up arrangements for practice it is the duty of all concerned to ensure that it does not degenerate into a mere technical trial of the firing machinery. On the contrary, the points to be emphasised are mobility, leadership, and correct tactical methods of handling detachments and guns.

The schemes at a practice camp should be so designed as to impress this point of view in a forcible manner on the commanders and personnel of machine-gun sections. The necessity of getting the full value out of their guns from a tactical point of view must be driven home until correct tactical action has become almost instinctive with both officers and men, and can be taken without hesitation or delay.

If in the actual course of practice men can be made to realise their own mistakes so clearly that they are never likely to repeat them, we may say that a practice camp has fulfilled its main object. For in such a case more good has been done than could be produced by any formal conference or criticism. A few examples will now be given to illustrate suitable methods of drawing up and carrying out practice schemes on the above lines. Particular attention will be devoted to fire against small or difficult targets, such as infantry firing lines in extended order. This is done with the express object of elucidating the necessity and importance of employing machine-gun fire to attack objectives, against which the full fire effect cannot be exerted. The fire superiority in the infantry combat is of decisive importance, and if it is to be obtained, such targets as those above-mentioned will very often have to be engaged by machine-guns.

I.

How to Draw Up and Carry Out a Practice Scheme.

Object of the Scheme.

Instruction in the correct choice of a target on tactical grounds, as well as the study of the disposition of the hostile firing lines with a view to obtaining flanking fire, and in giving clear orders for producing the maximum fire effect in the manner desired.

General Idea of a Scheme.

The scheme should be so drawn up as to produce a situation in which it is above all necessary to obtain a superiority of fire against the most important points of the enemy's front. The means of doing so are partly of a technical and partly of a tactical nature.

One technical method would be to increase the rate of fire of the separate individuals in the infantry firing line : but the employment of this method is very closely limited.

For although in peace conditions specially selected marksmen may have succeeded in firing 10 or more rounds a minute without loss of efficiency, it must be remembered that this will hardly be the case in war. The efficiency of men in battle, who, after many hardships, are called on to engage difficult targets, will be very different. It must also be remembered that a man can only carry a certain limited amount of ammunition.

Men who have used up all their rounds before they are within 600 yards of the enemy are of little more use than the dead or wounded. Ammunition supply from the rear is a problem which, in spite of many attempts, has not yet been satisfactorily solved.

Increase of the rate of fire must therefore be sought by tactical methods and by pushing more rifles into the combat. But there are limits also to this method of reinforcement, even when there is no lack of reserves available.

If the firing line is so closely packed that the men cannot use their firearms to the best advantage, we are only making the enemy a present of an excellent target. It is, however, always possible largely to increase the fire capacity of any part of our front by reinforcing it with machine-guns. A machine-gun hardly takes up more room in the front than four or five rifles. These four or five men, often very insufficiently protected, would be capable of delivering a fire of from 16 to 20 rounds a minute. A machine-gun detachment, protected by the gun shields from the hostile fire, is capable of firing some 300 rounds in an equal period of time. Actually, such a rate of fire would seldom be attained. If, however, the detachment is thoroughly conversant with the mechanism of the weapon, and if the fire discipline and training leaves nothing to be desired, the actual results obtained will not fall far short of those which are theoretically possible. In any case a machine-gun will always bring a far greater increase of fire power than will be brought by rifles occupying the same frontage. Also the pattern made by the fire of a machine-gun will, both in peace and war, be much closer and more uniform than that made by a group of riflemen. Hence machine-guns are peculiarly suitable for use in all situations in which it is imperative temporarily to silence or subdue the fire of the enemy, and, therefore, generally speaking, for use in obtaining fire superiority in the infantry fire fight. But it is not enough to recognise that machine-guns enable us to obtain a superiority of fire power, we must also consider where and how this superiority is to be applied.

The distribution of the fire front on a large scale is the duty of the higher leaders. If, however, owing to circumstances the fire front has not been thus apportioned, the suitable distribution of fire is a test of the tactical knowledge of the commander immediately concerned. If it is a question of intensifying the fire over any allotted or selected portion of the hostile front, care must be taken to avoid any cut-and-dried method of carrying out the task. For instance, if a commander simply directs his machine-gun detachments to come into action wherever they find room with a view to intensifying the fire, he will not be bringing the whole possible effect of his guns to bear against the enemy. It is quite conceivable that machine-guns acting under such instructions might come into action in places where they would be exposed to the full effect of the enemy's most destructive fire. In doing so they would be simply playing into his hands. The consideration of available space is not by any means invariably a determining factor in questions of reinforcement by machine-guns. In most cases the chief object to be aimed at is to distribute the guns so as to obtain a flanking or cross fire against certain definite portions of the hostile front. The best prospects of success are afforded by bringing flanking fire to bear on certain sections of the enemy's front, or by directing the convergent fire of scattered guns against a weak point in his position, or by concentrating the fire on spots which are thickly occupied by his troops. To apply fire in such a manner postulates a thorough study of the disposition of the hostile firing line. It must be known which portions of his line are especially hindering our advance, and against which parts of his front it is possible to fire from two or more directions.

When these matters have been duly appreciated, clear and definite orders, which leave no doubt in the mind of any subordinate as to the action expected of him, must be issued. Such a routine order as " Reinforce the fire of the line from X to Z," will never be sufficient : a definite task must be given. For instance: "'A' company has established itself from C to D, you will engage the enemy's line from E to F in order to cover the advance of 'B' company." Or "the machine-gun section will come into action behind that hedge and keep the enemy between the red house and the oak tree under fire, in order to facilitate the advance of 'C' company." Or "the left flank of 'D' company has come under heavy fire from that copse. Take your gun to that haystack and open rapid fire on the copse." In short, a definite task must be given to every unit instead of formal orders or generalities. It is in accordance with these principles that the general idea of a scheme should be evolved. We will now proceed to consider a special idea or problem at a practice camp, and how it can best be solved. This will also involve a consideration of the particular points in fire tactics which the camp commandant wishes the execution of his scheme to illustrate. Questions of fire discipline or fire effect can, of course, in due subordination to the scheme be worked in.

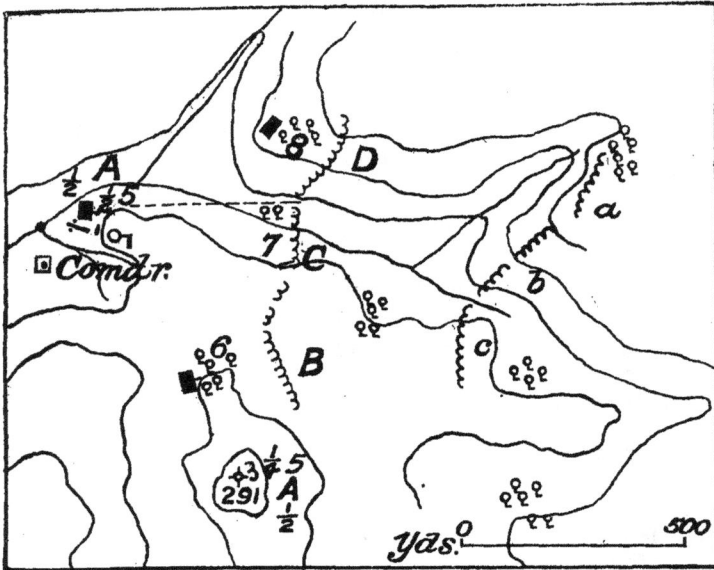

Target $a = 60$ ⎫ Figures coloured greenish grey lying down for
     ,, $b = 40$ ⎬ the most part under cover.
     ,, $c = 70$ ⎭

PRACTICE SCHEME (*see sketch*).

Carried out by an infantry machine-gun section. A battalion of infantry also took part in the scheme, but fired with blank cartridge only. The weather was sultry and the sun hot, there was a light breeze from the right, and the fall of the bullets could be seen.

Situation.

Our battalion advancing eastward has encountered the enemy (see sketch). It has deployed three and a half out of its four companies* and has a half company and the machine-gun section in reserve. The enemy's fire remains unsubdued, and a decisive attack is as yet inadvisable.

Task to be carried out and information received.

The commander of the machine-gun section and the officer in command of the reserve were standing by the side of the battalion commander (represented by the camp commandant). They were

* The peace strength of an Austrian battalion consists of four companies of 100 men each.

given at least ten minutes to examine the ground and to appreciate the situation. During this time the two officers were told how the situation arose, how long (half an hour) the fight had been in progress, what the effect of the fire had been on either side, and that the battalion commander had decided to drive the attack home as quickly as possible. As soon as the two officers had been fully informed on these points, the camp commandant (representing the battalion commander) gave orders that the reserve half company should reinforce the left wing of the firing line and drive the attack home. The commander of the machine-guns was ordered to prepare and support the attack. It must be noted that in war far more precise orders as to position and target would have to be issued here; for instructional purposes, however, the machine-gun commander was left free to act as he thought best.

Action taken by the machine-gun commander.

He selected the position shown on the sketch and issued the following orders, "Nos. 1 and range-finders to me, shields to the front, off loads." After reaching the position he gave "Target, enemy's firing line from *a* to *c* (pointing out landmarks), range 600 yards." He got this range by asking the infantry. The distribution of the target was as follows. The portion of front marked "c" to the right-hand gun; the portions marked "b" and "a" to the left-hand gun. On observing a number of shots falling short in front of the target the commander gave "range 650 yards, independent fire." There was a breakdown at the left-hand gun, which remained out of action for about one minute. The No. 1 of the right-hand gun took it upon himself to alter the range to 600, with the result that a large number of rounds again fell short of the target. From the receipt of the first order to the first shot 11½ minutes elapsed; from the first shot to cease fire 3 minutes; a total of 14½ minutes.

The right-hand gun fired 375 rounds, *i.e.*, 125 a minute. The left gun fired 206 rounds, *i.e.*, 69 a minute. Total number of rounds fired was 581.

Results of practice.

The left-hand gun fired at two targets, viz., "a" which consisted of 60 dummies, and "b" which consisted of 40 dummies. At target "a" 23 hits were obtained on 11 dummies, percentage of target destroyed 18·3. At target "b" 2 hits were obtained on 2 dummies, percentage of target destroyed ·5.

The right-hand gun fired at the target "c" which consisted of 70 dummies. No hits were obtained. Altogether 25 hits were obtained on 13 dummies out of 170. Percentage of total targets destroyed was 7·6. All the hits obtained were got by the left-hand gun, which therefore destroyed 12·1 per cent. of the total targets presented.

CONFERENCE.

Choice of target.—The situation and the orders of the battalion commander showed that the main attack was to be made on the left flank. We may assume that the hostile fire from the front "c" is kept down by our "B" company, assisted by the section of "A" com-

pany shown on the hill; it cannot therefore be turned against our left
flank advance. So there is no particular object in turning the fire of
the machine-guns on to "c," which is for the moment the least
important part, tactically speaking, of the hostile front. The portions
" a " and " b," on the other hand, are of great importance. To attack
the targets offered by the enemy in the order of their tactical
importance, is a *sine quâ non* for the successful employment of
machine-guns in battle. It is useless to try to cover every target
shown, with the fire of two machine guns. Such action, only
dissipates power and decreases the effect produced.

If, in a practice scheme, we provide more targets than the machine-
gun commander can effectively engage in the time allowed, and if we
thus force him to make a choice between targets of varying tactical
importance, we are giving ourselves every chance of really driving
home those principles which have just been enumerated. In this
case the machine-gun commander, once his attention had been
directed to the different tactical importance of the three targets, was
able to realize and point out his own errors.

After the choice of targets " a " and " b " has been admitted to be
correct, the question arises of the best positions for the guns.

Choice of positions.—On examining the line of the hostile front, it
is to be observed that the fronts " a " and " b " form a re-entrant
angle. Consequently the enemy can bring a heavy crossfire on to the
zone of ground over which D company and the half of A company
(now in reserve) will have to advance. It is, therefore, the duty of
the machine-gun section to keep these portions of the enemy's line
under the most effective fire possible, preferably under a flank or
cross fire. This therefore will be the chief condition to be satisfied
in selecting positions for the guns.

The position actually taken up (see sketch), does not fulfil this
condition. The guns can only bring a frontal fire to bear against " a "
and " b," while they themselves are liable to come under cross fire
from " a " and " c."

The rising ground at point 291 (see sketch), where a section of
No. 5 Company is posted, offers a much more suitable position. For,
from that position, it will be possible to bring enfilade fire to bear
against " b " at 900 to 1,000 yards, and against " a " at 1,000 to 1,150
yards, and thus keep down the cross fire to which our left flank
advance will be exposed.

Another advantage of this position lies in the fact that the
advance can be continuously protected by covering fire up to the
final charge. Our regulations say on this subject : " It is particularly
advantageous to keep the point chosen for attack under the fire of
machine-guns, by posting them either on a flank, or on a height from
which they can support the attack up to the last moment without the
necessity of changing position."

In the instance under consideration, both the machine-gun
commander and other officers who were present admitted that they
quite realized the truth of this principle now that it was objectively
pointed out to them, though they had previously failed to do so.
This admission was one of the most gratifying incidents of the
practice camp. It showed that we all pay too little attention to the
acquirement of a " tactical eye," and that we do not sufficiently

examine and analyze a hostile firing line from a tactical point of view. We should never let slip any opportunity of training ourselves in these matters. What has just been said on the subject of positions is naturally chiefly applicable to the particular instance under consideration. When working with a unit which has other troops on each side of it, machine-guns will of course have to come into action, behind or in the firing line of their own unit. Even in such cases excellent opportunities for effective action of a flanking nature will often present themselves, and under the cover of their shields machine-guns will be able to attack other portions of the enemy's line, than that which is immediately opposite to them.

Effect of the fire.—In the time given, it would have been possible for the two guns to fire 1,500 to 1,800 rounds. The actual number of rounds fired, 581, was far below the possible. The right gun only fired at the rate of 125 rounds a minute, the left gun at an even smaller rate, 69 rounds a minute, with the simple mechanism of our guns, breakdowns will be less common than in other armies which have more complicated weapons.

Breakdowns are often to be traced to want of training among the personnel of the detachment. When they occur at a practice camp they afford an opportunity for the men to practice repair of damage under a close approximation to service conditions. But they also show that ignorance of mechanism, or neglect in mechanical training, will have to be dearly paid for in war.

The slow rate of fire of the left-hand gun was not only due to the breakdown but also to the interruption of fire caused by numerous corrections in laying, made by No. 1. The pattern made by the gun is very close and it must therefore be laid very correctly, and hence corrections in laying are from time to time necessary. But the better the preparations before opening fire and the better the laying of the No. 1 the fewer and shorter will be the interruptions of fire caused by the necessity of making corrections. In the case under consideration the volume of fire delivered by the two guns was hardly greater than that of 30 or 40 riflemen. Such a result cannot be regarded as satisfactory.

Hits obtained.—The right hand gun made no hits. The hits, 25 in all, were all obtained by the left hand gun. The percentage of target destroyed, 12 per cent, was distinctly good; though the fact that only 13 dummies were hit, shows that the No. 1 of the gun did not distribute his fire sufficiently.

If we ask whether on the whole the task set to the machine-gun section was, or was not, efficiently carried out, the answer must be in the affirmative.

Considering that 11 out of 60 dummies occupying the part of the position " a " were put out of action by the machine-guns alone; and that further losses would have been inflicted by rifle fire, we cannot help coming to the conclusion that the attack against " a " would certainly have succeeded. The losses caused in " b " were not sufficient to ensure success at that point. Finally, it is quite clear that the results obtained were far below what might have been produced, if the tactical leading and distribution of fire had been better. Such a conclusion cannot but act as an incentive to further effort and study.

PART II.

THE INCREASE OF FIRE EFFECT WHICH CAN BE OBTAINED BY THE
SUITABLE USE OF MACHINE-GUNS IN THE DECISIVE INFANTRY FIRE
COMBAT, AS DETERMINED BY INSTRUCTIONAL PRACTICES.

It has already been shown (in Part 1) that the fire effect of
machine-guns considerably exceeds that of riflemen occupying the
same space as the guns. The exact extent, however, to which the
fire effect of a line of infantry can be increased by the employment
of machine-guns, is a matter on which opinions differ widely; and
opinicns are by no means unanimous, even among those who have
had most to do with machine-guns and their employment.

On this subject we may easily be led astray by deductions from
range practices, unless indeed these are drawn from a very large
number of instances.

Range practices are misleading, in so far as they bring to light
only the material, and not the moral, effect produced by machine-
guns. In considering the issue of the infantry fire fight the moral
effect of machine-guns must never be disregarded.

When we think of the heavy loss which can be caused by machine-
guns over a restricted area in a very short period of time we see that
the influence which they exert on an enemy must be very great.
Nor must we forget that the bullets which fail actually to hit have
also great moral effect if they go close to the enemy. They force him
down under cover, disturb his aim, and thus enable our own infantry
to fire more effectively. A short quotation from the experiences of a
Japanese officer may perhaps make this point clearer :—

> "Officers and men were profoundly impressed by the power
> of machine-guns. When an attack began they waited for the
> crackle of their own machine-guns with the same impatient
> expectation as that of a farmer for the first drops of rain in a dry
> and sultry summer. Everybody's spirits rose when the sound
> was heard, though nobody knew the actual effect, if any, which
> they were producing on the enemy ; the opening of the machine-
> guns was greeted with cheers, even the wounded rose to their
> feet and shouted 'Banzai!' I have often seen a situation
> completely alter, on the first tap-tap of the maxims."

Hence it is clear that material and moral effect interact on each
other, and it is not possible to ascertain with accuracy the exact
material effect produced in any particular instance.

Even when all the conditions favour the attainment of the highest
possible efficacy by a machine-gun, there is always one factor to be
considered, which can never be accurately determined beforehand,
that is, the effect of the enemy's fire.

Numerous instructional combined practices of infantry and machine-guns have been carried out at the School of Musketry with a view to showing the extent to which the fire effect of infantry can (but not necessarily would) be increased, by reinforcing them with machine-guns. A few out of many such examples are attached to illustrate the present article.

The experience obtained from the various combined practices shows clearly that the co-operation of machine-guns in the decisive struggle for fire superiority largely increases the chances of success of the infantry which possesses them, and adds greatly to the material effect of the fire. The result of the struggle for the fire superiority will often chiefly depend on the suitable or unsuitable employment of machine-guns (see examples 1 and 2, on plate facing page 18). It is, therefore, necessary to make a careful examination of the principles by which the employment of machine-guns in this phase of the combat should be guided.

Let us first consider the action of an infantry firing line. We may take it as a principle that each man fires at that point of the enemy's line which is immediately opposite to him. To switch the fire of an infantry line to a flank is a task which presents, even in peace, very great difficulties. In war it may be considered to be impossible. The only way of doing it is to form a new front by bringing up reserves. If it be desired to increase the fire effect of a firing line against a particular part of the enemy's line, the reinforcements must be brought up immediately opposite that part. But this principle does not hold good in the case of machine-guns. Infantry are prevented from firing to a flank by the fact that the men on each side of them mark their fire. There is no such impedient to the flank fire of machine-guns.

Passing orders regarding targets down an infantry firing line is a very slow, and often impossible, business ; such orders have to be passed on from individual to individual and are often misunderstood or altered in transmission. With a machine-gun detachment it is only necessary to give the orders to the two Numbers 1 of the guns. A commander can direct, control, concentrate, and disperse the fire of machine-guns even in the last stages of the combat, long after the control of the infantry fire has passed from his hands. He can give the machine-gun commander precise and detailed orders as to the targets he wishes him to engage. Thus the commander can follow the progress of the attack and direct fire to be turned on those portions of the enemy's line which form the greatest obstacle to the advance of his infantry.

We can therefore deduce the principle that machine-guns are specially adapted for switching on flank fire, and for such tasks as enfilading portions of the enemy's front, beating back local counter-attacks, and for support of advancing infantry, as well as for attacking detachments, reserves, etc., in rear of the enemy's front. These targets, by means of machine-gun fire, can be rapidly and effectively engaged without diverting the fire of the infantry from the enemy's immediate front (see example 3). Machine-gun detachments should, therefore, be able to change target to the front or flank with great celerity and furthermore to understand what targets should be engaged and why. Hence not only is great technical efficiency necessary, but also constant practise in appreciating tactical situations on the part of the Section Commanders and Numbers 1.

We have already shown that the correct choice of position is an essential condition for the successful co-operation of machine-guns in the decisive fire combat. From the preceding statements it is clear that the most favourable position is one from which fire can be turned on to all portions of the enemy's position, and from which the hostile reserves can be engaged before they reach the firing line. Often these conditions can only be fulfilled by a position in the firing line, and even then not always completely. Our regulations say " local fire superiority at the point where the final charge is to be delivered will sometimes be unobtainable without bringing the machine-guns into the firing line itself." Unless terrain or local conditions make it absolutely necessary, the vicinity of the firing line should be avoided in choosing a position. For, if a position away from the firing line be selected, the enemy is obliged to distribute his fire between the guns and the firing line (see example 4). Also an advance of the machine-guns into the firing line, unless carried out under cover, will generally be attended by considerable loss to the detachments. If such loss is, however, unavoidable, it must, as our regulations direct, be incurred without hesitation. Such necessity, however, will seldom arise ; as a rule the task of machine-guns during the struggle for fire superiority will be best fulfilled by occupying positions in rear of the firing line, from which fire can be directed on the enemy, either through gaps in the firing line or from elevations which permit of firing over the heads of the infantry. This possibility of firing over the heads of the infantry is one that should be constantly kept in mind by all commanders. In peace time such overhead fire is not permissible when ball cartridge is being used. Hence there is a danger that this method of fire may be neglected in war. Particular care should therefore be taken at all peace manœuvres where blank cartridge is used, to choose those positions in rear of the troops from which the best results can be obtained. It should be noted that the regulation which limits overhead fire to targets at 1,000 yards and over, with a minimum distance of 400 yards between men and guns, applies only to cases where all three are on the same horizontal plane. In cases where either the target or the guns are at some height above the troops, this rule does not apply. The prohibition in peace time applies only to ball cartridge, practice in firing with blank cartridge over infantry should be carried out on every available opportunity. Infantry can thus to a certain extent be accustomed to the conditions under which they would have to work in war. Finally a few remarks must be made about the cover which is afforded to machine-gun detachments by the gun shields. These enable the detachments to hold out even when in the firing line and exposed to very heavy fire from the enemy. The results obtained in the examples given on attached plate, show that machine-gun detachments when behind shields can be made to suffer heavily by enfilade or flank fire. To produce such an effect, however, careful preparation is necessary, and marksmen must be suitably posted by skilful and capable section or squad leaders.

It is often forgotten that the shields can be so arranged as to give protection against flank fire.

SUMMARY.

The undeniable increase of fire effect which can be obtained by the co-operation of the machine-guns during the fight for fire superiority may often be the deciding factor in the contest.

In this phase of the conflict machine-guns should chiefly engage those targets such as reserves which can be taken in flank, etc., which, owing to want of time or opportunity, are neglected by the infantry. The infantry may be unable for tactical reasons to change targets, or it may be impossible to pass the necessary orders to and along the firing line. The situations are few in which it is desirable to push the guns actually into the firing line. As a rule they should be posted in gaps in the line, on the flanks, or in elevated positions behind the firing line from which they can fire over it.

EXAMPLES. (*With* 4 *diagrams.*)*

The following examples are given to indicate the general method in which schemes for instructional field firing should be drawn up and executed.

The remarks on each example show the sense in which results may be used for illustration and instruction. Many lessons of various sorts can be drawn from such practices, according to the point of view from which they are regarded.

However desirable this may be for an individual who is making a special study of the subject, it is most important at the conference which immediately follows the practice, to avoid being discursive, and to confine the criticism and discussion to the most important points at issue. Otherwise these may be obscured or even entirely lost sight of. It is a matter of no small difficulty though of great importance to single out the really essential points and impress them on the audience at the conference, even at the cost of suppressing many interesting details and points of minor importance. The direction of the conference lies in the hands of the Commandant, whose duty it is to conduct the criticism and discussion on the lines above mentioned.

EXAMPLE I. (*See diagram* 1.)

Increase of fire effect obtained by putting a machine-gun into the firing line.

The targets were arranged to represent a combat between two firing lines, one (A) without a machine-gun, the other (B) with a machine-gun. In both cases the line was in close formation and the range was 800 yards.

Target A, which consisted of 70 dummies lying in the open, was attacked by 70 rifles and a machine-gun. 1,608 shots were fired in $3\frac{1}{2}$ minutes, viz.: 1,205 shots by the infantry and 403 by the machine-gun. There were 72 hits on 42 figures, giving a percentage of hits to shots fired of 4·4, while 60 per cent. of the dummies were hit.

Target B, which consisted of 70 dummies as above and 5 dummies

* For diagrams, see plate at the end of the book.

behind shields representing a machine-gun detachment, was attacked by 70 riflemen. Time of firing was 3½ minutes. 1,034 shots were fired. 29 hits were obtained on 24 dummies. Percentage of hits to shots fired was 2, while 32 per cent. of the dummies were hit.

The two practices were simultaneous; as each hit was obtained, one of the opposite firing party was put out of action.

The time, 3½ minutes, was arrived at by sounding the cease fire as soon as one target had suffered about twice as much loss as the other. The lines of fire, as anticipated by the camp staff, are shown on the diagram thus (——————•). As a matter of fact the machine-gun attacked only the left part of the target to which it was opposed.

Firing party B had a superior firing power of 403 cartridges, directly due to the machine-gun. The infantry of Party B fired 171 more cartridges than the infantry of Party A. This is attributable to the fact of the machine-gun putting so many of Party A out of action during the firing.

But the success of Party B was not chiefly due to its larger consumption of cartridges. It was due to the good practice made by the machine-gun against the left of target A. The effect would have been much greater if the Number 1 of the gun had distributed his fire better and also attacked the right of the target. The diagram shows that twelve dummies received two or more hits apiece.

Conclusion.—A machine-gun well handled, from a technical and tactical point of view, can turn the scale in a fight between two infantry firing lines in close order.

EXAMPLE II. (*See diagram 2.*)

An illustration of the fact that a firing line with a machine-gun can sometimes be defeated by a firing line without one.

Targets were arranged and shooting took place on the same lines as in the previous example. The range was 950 yards.

Target A, which consisted of 100 dummies lying in close order, was attacked by Party B, consisting of 100 riflemen and a machine-gun. Time of firing, 2 minutes. Number of shots fired, 1,725, *i.e.*, 1,135 by the infantry and 590 by the machine-gun. Hits, 34. Dummies hit, 29. Percentage of hits to shots fired, 2. Percentage of dummies hit, 29.

Target B, consisting of 100 dummies similar to the above and 5 dummies lying behind shields to represent a machine-gun detachment, was attacked by Party A, consisting of 100 riflemen. Time of firing, 2 minutes. Shots fired, 1,391. Hits, 52. Dummies hit, 46. Percentage of hits to shots fired, 3·8. Percentage of dummies hit, 44.

The procedure followed was the same as in the previous example, *i.e.*, a rifleman was put out of action whenever a hit was made on a dummy.

The machine-gun of Party B shot too short, and had not found the range when the cease fire sounded. The additional fire power of 590 cartridges, which the possession of a machine-gun gave to Party B, was of no use to them, as the machine-gun never got the range.

The result of the firing shows that the firing line of Party A must have ranged more correctly and fired more accurately than that of Party B. Therefore the numbers of Party B decreased more rapidly than those of Party A. Consequently Party A was able to fire 256 more cartridges than Party B. The result of the shooting was not at all what had been expected by the Directing Staff. It was exceptional, and the particular lesson which the practice had been designed to exemplify could not be drawn. But in such cases the practice must not be considered as a failure. A commandant must be prepared for surprises of this sort and must be able to make even negative results instructive.

For instance, in this particular case a good line to follow at the conference would be to emphasize the following points : Point out that technical mistakes in fire discipline, ranging and gun-drill may nullify the results of the most skilful tactical dispositions. That infantry must have due regard to machine-gun fire, without dreading it. That fear of the machine-gun is a thing to be fought against. That machine-guns often make a lot of noise without doing the slightest damage. Show the hits on the dummies representing the machine-gun detachment, and remark on the necessity of careful arrangements for putting them out of action. Point out that it is the duty of section and squad leaders to tell off special parties and individuals to keep up a flanking fire on machine-gun detachments, and on men or animals bringing up fresh supplies of ammunition.

EXAMPLE III. (*See diagram* 3.)

Illustrating the suitability of machine-guns for rapidly engaging fresh targets and changing from one target to another.

Two exactly similar sets of targets at ranges varying from 800 to 1,000 yards were successively engaged by (*a*) a section of infantry (35 men), and by (*b*) a similar section of infantry and a machine-gun.

The targets consisted in each case of 35 dummies lying without cover and visible during the whole duration of the practice, *i.e.*, $1\frac{1}{2}$ minutes.

In addition 18 moving targets (Nos. I and II in the diagram) appeared and advanced half a minute after the opening of fire, remaining visible for half a minute and then disappeared. As they disappeared 17 similar dummies (Nos. II and IV in the diagram) appeared and advanced for the remaining half-minute.

The first practice (*a*) was carried out by 35 riflemen.

The second practice (*b*) by 35 riflemen and a machine-gun. Orders in both cases were to keep up continuous fire on any portion of the hostile line which was lying down and firing, and to prevent any advance.

Results of the first practice (*a*) were :—

> Rounds fired, 409. Hits, 24. Dummies hit, 18.
> Percentage of hits to rounds fired, 5·8.
> Percentage of dummies hit, 25·7.

Results of the second practice (*b*) were :—

> Rounds fired, 860 (*i.e.*, 475 by the infantry, 385 by the machine-gun).

Hits, 60. Dummies hit, 29.
Percentage of hits to rounds fired, 7.
Percentage of dummies hit, 41.

If in both series we confine our attention to the advancing dummies, we find in each case a similar result, *i.e.*, on targets I to IV in (*a*) 13 dummies hit, and in (*b*) 14 dummies hit. There is, therefore, nothing to choose between the two in the execution of the second part of the orders, *i.e.*, to prevent any advance.

But in order to achieve this result, it was, in the first series (*a*), necessary to neglect the first part of the orders issued, *i.e.*, to keep the recumbent part of the hostile line under continuous fire. In order to get their 13 hits every rifle in Party A had to be turned on to the advancing dummies.

In the second series (*b*), the duty of engaging the advancing dummies was allotted to the machine-gun, while the infantry kept the recumbent dummies under continuous fire. This is very clearly shown by examination of the hits on the targets, *i.e.*, only 5 of the recumbent dummies hit in the first series (*a*), as against 15 in the second series (*b*).

It must be mentioned that the practice was carried out by men who had been carefully trained in changing targets quickly, and warning had been given that disappearing targets were to be expected.

That the infantry in the second series (*b*) fired more rounds than the infantry in the first series (*a*) is to be attributed to the fact that in case (*b*) they never had to change target, while in case (*a*) two changes of target were necessary.

Conclusion.—We see the advantage of using machine-guns when quick changes of target are necessary, especially for repulsing the advance of reserves. In actual warfare the advantage would be greater, for it would then be far more difficult to get an infantry firing line to change target with speed and precision.

EXAMPLE IV. (*See diagram* 4.)

Showing how fire effect is influenced by posting machine-guns (*a*) behind the infantry firing line (*b*), in the infantry firing line.

The number of dummies was the same both in series (*a*) and in series (*b*), *i.e.*, 50 falling plates representing recumbent figures and 10 recumbent dummies without cover representing the detachments of two machine-guns. In each series 45 riflemen fired for 5 minutes. In series (*a*) the results were—Rounds fired, 1,143 ; hits, 26 ; dummies hit, 24 ; percentage of hits to rounds fired, 2·3 ; percentage of dummies hit, 40.

In series (*b*) the results were—rounds fired, 1,279 ; hits, 49 ; dummies hit, 37 ; percentage of hits to rounds fired, 3·9 ; percentage of dummies hit, 62.

As regards the machine-gun target, the result of series (*a*) when 7 dummies were hit was better than that of series (*b*) when only 4 were hit.

The good result in series (*a*) was, however, only obtained at the cost of decreased effect against the infantry dummies, of which only 17 were hit as against 33 in series (*b*).

The necessity of distributing the fire and of firing at two different ranges caused the rate of fire in series (a) to be slower. In series (a) 136 cartridges less than in series (b) were fired. This represents a considerable loss of fire power, directly caused by the separation of the hostile machine-gun from the firing line.

The counter effect produced by the fire of the machine-gun would certainly have been smaller at 1,300 yards than at 800 yards. But how much smaller would depend mainly on the degree of accuracy in the estimation of the range on the part of the machine-gun commander. Faults in estimating ranges are just as possible at 800 yards as at 1,300 yards, as can be seen from Example II. On the other hand, a commander can much more easily influence and direct the action of machine-guns if they are well away from the firing line. A position in the firing line makes it difficult for him to do so.

Machine-guns should, therefore, as a rule be placed behind the firing line, especially when local conditions are favourable; for instance, when the enemy is posted on a ridge, when it is possible to fire from above one's own infantry firing line, and in many other similar cases.

PART III.

THE HANDLING OF AN INFANTRY MACHINE-GUN DETACHMENT AT A COMBINED FIELD FIRING PRACTICE.

The tactical handling of an infantry machine-gun detachment which took part in an infantry field firing practice will now be described.

The scheme was made as simple as possible in order to prevent complications and conventionalities, and attempts to be dodgy and clever. The lie of the range was such that flanking fire could only be employed at a very small angle to the main line of fire. For instructional reasons, the machine-gun commander, the initial situation having been explained to him and having received general directions for action from the instructional staff, received no further orders. The manner in which the machine-gun commander appreciated the various situations, his decisions, and the action and lines of fire that resulted therefrom, are described from what actually happened and from explanations at the conference. They are not put forward as patterns to be imitated, but to exemplify the sort of thing which actually occurs and in order to arouse discussion.

The distribution of the fire of Nos. 3 and 4 Companies is shown by dotted lines. The distribution might certainly have been better; this was pointed out by the officers themselves, who were responsible for it. Distribution of infantry fire is a difficult business even in peace; it requires constant practice and unremitting attention. Indeed, we must not place too much reliance on its possibility or efficacy in war, though this does not absolve us from the duty of constant effort in peace.

Nos. 1 and 2 Companies shot with blank cartridge. The instructions given to them by the instructional staff were such as to necessitate their crossing the covered part of the ground (*see* sketch No. 1) with great rapidity. They were then made (by threatening their left flank with attack) to assume a very cautious and hesitating attitude. A situation was thus produced in which the remainder (*i.e.*, those shooting with ball cartridge) were supported on both flanks, and were obliged to occupy when deployed the whole breadth of the range.

The patch of wood S.S.E. of Point 152 was to be considered as impassable for troops.

The course of the operations is not described in detail; the narrative is intended only to explain and elucidate the decisions and action of the machine-gun commander.

Phase 1.

Phase 2.

Phase 1.

Initial situation. Information and instructions issued to the battalion (No. 1).

Our own main body, whose left flank is marked by a flag, is attacking the ridge to the S. and S.E., which is held by an imaginary enemy.

No. 1 Battalion, with an infantry machine-gun detachment, is echeloned to the left rear as a reserve (as shown on Sketch 1).

Phase 2.

Hostile forces are seen advancing over the crest of Hospital Hill; their advance seems to be directed against the left wing of our main body.

Machine-gun Commander's View of the Situation.

These forces must at all costs be prevented from interfering with the action of our main body.

Machine-gun Commander's Decision.

To open fire on the advancing enemy at the same time as Nos. 3 and 4 Companies.

Phase 3.

The fire of Nos. 3 and 4 Companies and of the machine-gun detachment forces the enemy to change front towards the Leitha Canal and to form line between the small wood west of the quarry and the cemetery. His fire is at first somewhat wild and irregular, but increases in precision as time goes on. The battalion commander orders Nos. 4 and 3 Companies to attack over the zone of ground bounded on the W. by the stream and a line thence to the Signal Station, and on the E. by a line from the small wood (400 paces S. of Point 152), to the W. edge of the quarry. Nos. 1 and 2 Companies to attack E. of this latter line.

No. 4 Company begins the advance, partially covered by the two thickets shown in the sketch. No. 3 Company keeps up a heavy covering fire.

Machine-gun Commander's View of the Situation.

The enemy has come under fire and has been obliged to form front towards the battalion. I shall not get much result by opening fire at such a long range against the hostile firing line, which is lying down. It is possible that the enemy, when he has recovered from the first effects of our fire, which took him by surprise, will advance again.

Machine-gun Commander's Decision.

Not to fire, but to make all preparations for opening fire.

Phase 4.

Parts of No. 4 Company have worked through to the second thicket. No. 3 Company attempted to advance over the open ground in front of it, but was beaten back.

Phase 3.

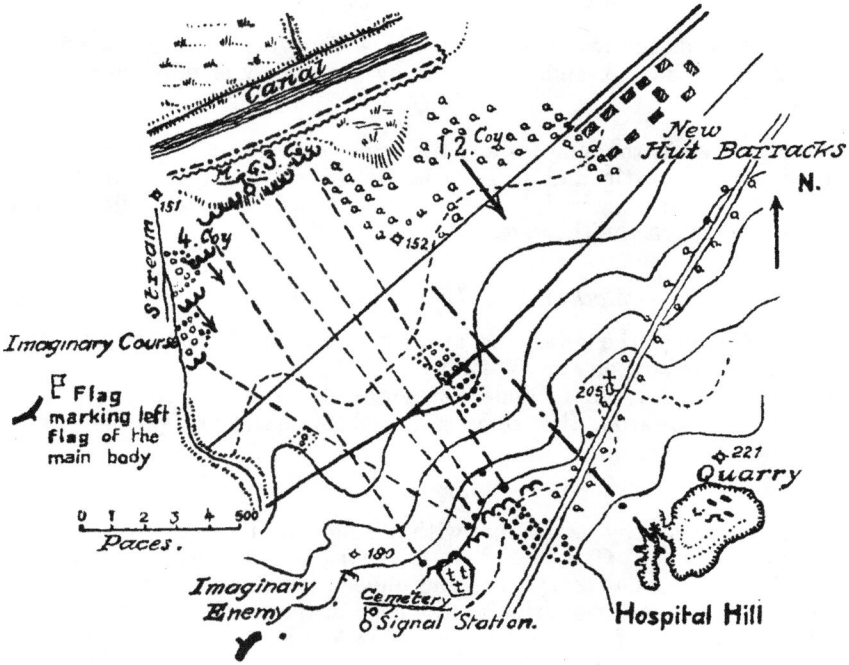

Phase 4.

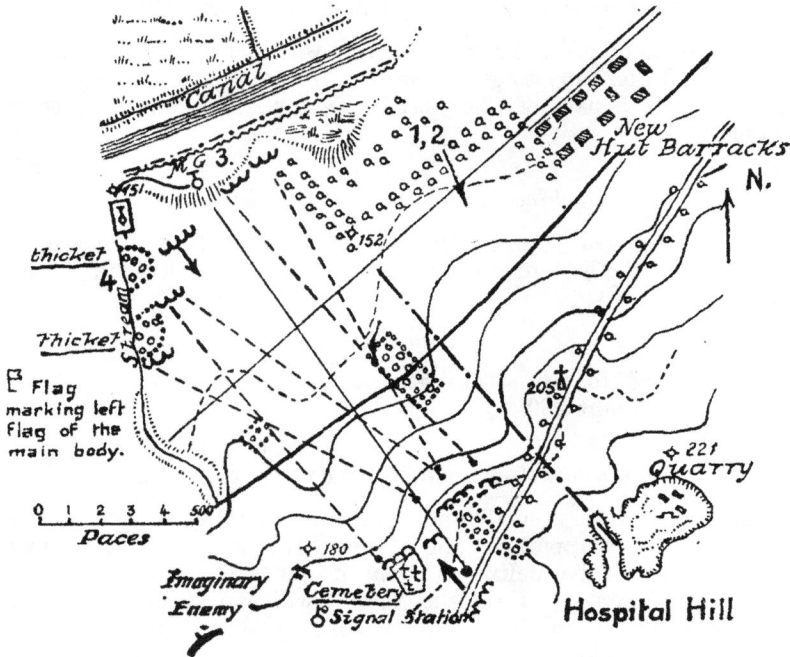

Machine-gun Commander's View of the Situation.

As soon as the rear portions of No. 4 Company advance they will mask my guns. A sudden attack by the enemy is possible at any moment.

My range is too long for any really decisive effect. I should like to advance a little, and if I do so I shall move under cover of the thickets. The danger is that the enemy will attack while I am moving through the thickets.

Machine-gun Commander's Decision.

To advance the guns, one at a time, to a position on the edge of the front thicket (on the W. flank).

While this is being done a reserve of the enemy is seen to be advancing towards the cemetery, and is attacked by the rear machine-gun.

Phase 5.

No. 4 Company is in line with its right on the southernmost of the two thickets. One half of No. 3 Company is following behind on its right rear as a reserve, keeping under cover by the stream. The machine-guns are in position on the edge of the southernmost thicket. The other half of No. 3 Company, further E., is trying to advance over the open ground. It is evidently in considerable difficulty and has suffered a good deal of loss.

Machine-gun Commander's View of the Situation.

In order to obtain the fire superiority we must enable the eastern half of No. 3 Company to get forward. We must try and keep down the fire of that part of the hostile line which is stopping their advance.

Machine-gun Commander's Decision.

To open enfilade fire on the eastern portion of the hostile line, and thus help the half of No. 3 Company on the east flank to get forward.

Phase 6.

A section of No. 4 Company has made a rush and got into a little copse N.W. of Point 180.

Machine-gun Commander's View of the Situation.

The copse is very small and does not give much cover. It is a valuable point of support for the attack. If it is to be held a heavy fire will have to be delivered from it, for the enemy can bring converging fire on it. From the copse it will be possible to support a further advance, and to fire at that part of the hostile line which the copse now masks.

Phase 5.

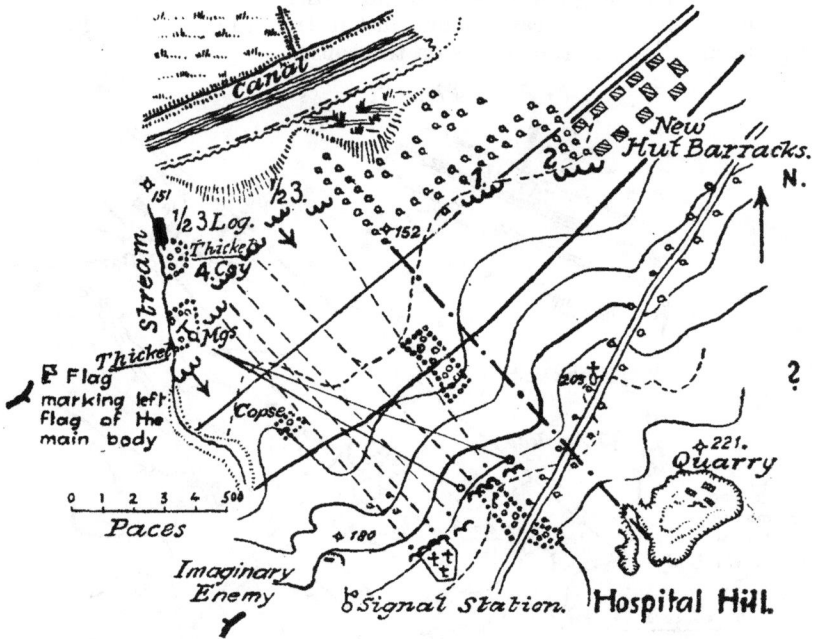

Phase 6.

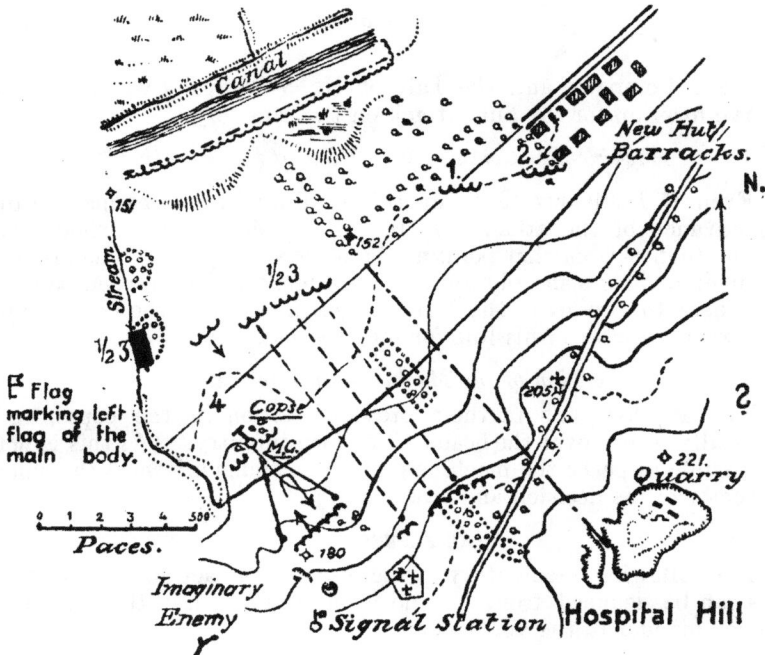

Machine-gun Commander's Decision.

To advance the guns rapidly to the copse.

The movement is carried out just in time to enable the guns to repulse an attack of the enemy on the copse.

Phase 7.

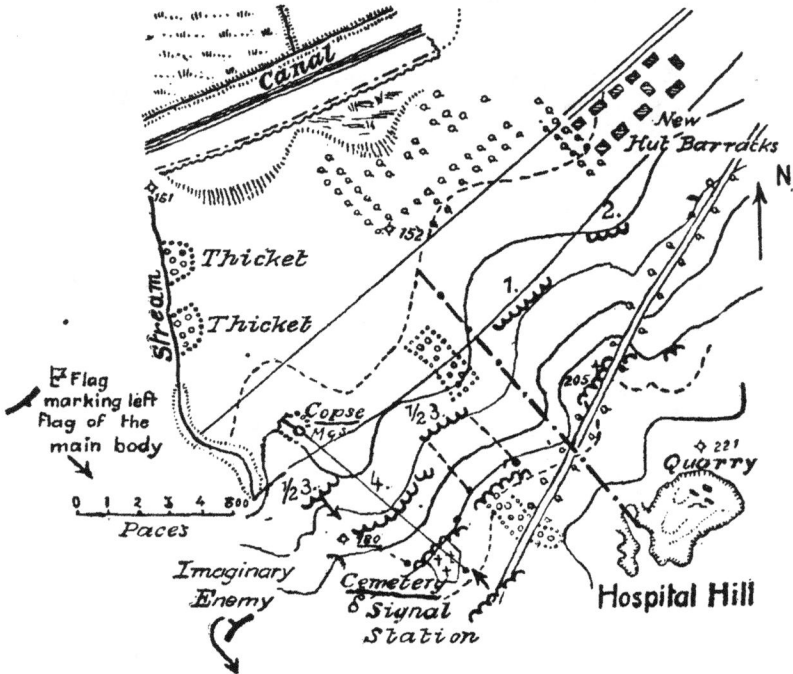

No. 4 Company and the half of No. 3 Company which was in reserve form up for the final attack on the cemetery.

Machine-gun Commander's View of the Situation.

Even if I advance to Point 180 my fire will soon be masked by the advance of the attack. It is quite probable that I should be unable to fire from that point at the decisive moment. The ground is convex and rises sharply towards the enemy, so I shall soon be able from here to fire over the heads of our infantry at the hostile line and sweep the rear of his line for reserves, etc.

Decision of the Machine-gun Commander.

To leave his guns in their present position in the copse, and eventually to fire over the heads of his own infantry. (As this is not permissible in peace the machine-gun commander informed the chief instructor of his decision and ceased fire.)

CONFERENCE.

The following elementary principles for the action of machine-guns can be deduced from the decisions and action of the machine-gun commander in the above example.

Machine-guns are not intended for action, independent of their own infantry.

They must be regarded solely as an auxiliary weapon to be used to increase fire effect as the tactical situation may demand ; in this particular case, in order to enable the whole of the infantry to deploy and advance.

The sphere of operation of machine-guns is not confined to the particular target which at any given moment they may be attacking, but extends over the whole zone of action of that body of infantry to which they are allotted. Machine-gun commanders must not let themselves be hypnotized by the action of the troops in their immediate vicinity ; they must regard the action as a whole, and seize any opportunity of influencing the *general* course of the whole conflict in a favourable sense.

This leads us to the conclusion that a machine-gun commander, if he is to co-operate successfully with the troops to which he is attached, must have an intimate knowledge of the tactical methods employed by those troops, and of their needs from moment to moment in each and every tactical situation.

He must be able, owing to his tactical knowledge, not only to recognize, but to anticipate tactical situations. Without this power of anticipation, founded on experience, knowledge and study, he will usually find that his action is too late to be of value.

Consequently, a machine-gun commander, in a simple tactical exercise of the nature described, may be justly expected from the moment the initial situation is given, to have a good general idea of the course which events are likely to take.

In this case he might fairly be expected to be prepared for the advance to closer ranges, for counter-attacks on the part of the enemy ; to recognize in due time that the advance of his infantry on the west flank owing to the ground would be easier and quicker than that of the infantry on the east flank. He should have deduced therefrom that he would probably be called on to enfilade the enemy's east flank despite the fact that it offers a somewhat difficult target with a view to keeping down hostile fire over the open ground to be crossed on the east flank.

He should also be prepared, if the final attack succeeds, to follow up the retreating enemy with a well-directed fire, and to establish himself in a strong position at the cemetery, and use that important position as a supporting point from which to beat back a possible offensive return on the part of the enemy.

The Russo-Japanese war shows us that the debated possession of such valuable supporting points was often only finally decided when one side or the other succeeded in occupying the contested point with machine-guns.

We can all remember very many situations in war in which a commander of no greater importance than a machine-gun commander has been obliged to make decisions and take action of far-reaching importance to the whole course of a great battle.

A machine-gun commander must, therefore, have a thorough tactical education and knowledge, not only of the action of small units, but also of that of large bodies of troops. Take, for instance, the case of a machine-gun detachment with an advanced guard.

C

Here it may be necessary to renounce the opportunity of firing at the most tempting and important targets because the matter of real tactical importance is to seize and occupy certain important points, the possession of which will be of the utmost value to the main body following behind. Here the machine-gun commander will have to forego chances of brilliant personal distinction in the interest of the army as a whole.

Again, let us take the case of a retreat after a battle. Here the machine-gun commander will probably have to draw on his own tactical experience in order to know approximately the order in which the various bodies of troops will retire, and what measures the pursuing enemy is likely to take. The action of his detachment will depend almost entirely on the correctness of his judgment founded on tactical knowledge. Self-sacrifice will very likely be necessary; whether the sacrifice is useful or profitable will depend on the extent of his tactical knowledge.

The capacity for rightly appreciating a tactical situation is the result, first and foremost, of long experience. Hence only well-tried officers of considerable seniority should be appointed to the command of machine-guns. It is evident that all the above remarks as to the necessity of tactical knowledge apply with equal force, though in a smaller sphere, to the Nos. 1 of machine-guns. Swift and intelligent obedience on the part of subordinates cannot be expected unless they understand the circumstances in which they are acting. Nos. 1 should, therefore, be instructed on every possible opportunity in tactical principles and methods, and should be encouraged to pass on their knowledge to those below them. The necessity of tactical knowledge has been emphasized, but it is also impossible to lay too much stress on the necessity of technical training in handling the gun, shooting, repairing breakdowns, etc. Tactical skill is useless unless technical proficiency is present.

The following distribution of various subjects at the conference held after the particular practice which has been described may serve as a rough guide in similar cases :—

The camp commandant dealt with the general tactical considerations.

The musketry instructor dealt with musketry questions, hits on targets, technical handling of the gun, ranging, etc. The machine-gun commander described his actions in detail, his arrangements for supply of ammunition, for using the pack animals, and the action of his Nos. 1. The Nos. 1 described what took place at their guns, the behaviour of the various individual numbers, etc.

The general object of the series of articles on machine-guns of which this is the last will by this time be obvious. They are intended to emphasize the necessity of obtaining the maximum tactical effect from the enormous fire power which technical skill and training can get out of the gun. An attempt has been made to show that in every kind of training and practice up to and including combined field firing, just as much attention should be paid to the tactical handling of machine-guns as has been hitherto devoted to the improvement of their technical efficiency.

EXPLANATORY NOTE:- *The black dots represent hits .*
The black lines_____• represent
the lines of fire anticipated by
the Camp Staff.

1.— INCREASE OF FIRE EFFECT OBTAINED BY PUTTING A MACHINE GUN INTO THE FIRING LINE.

Targets represent a combat between two firing lines, men in close order,
One firing line (b) has a machine gun; the other (a) has not.
Conditions of firing etc. otherwise similar.

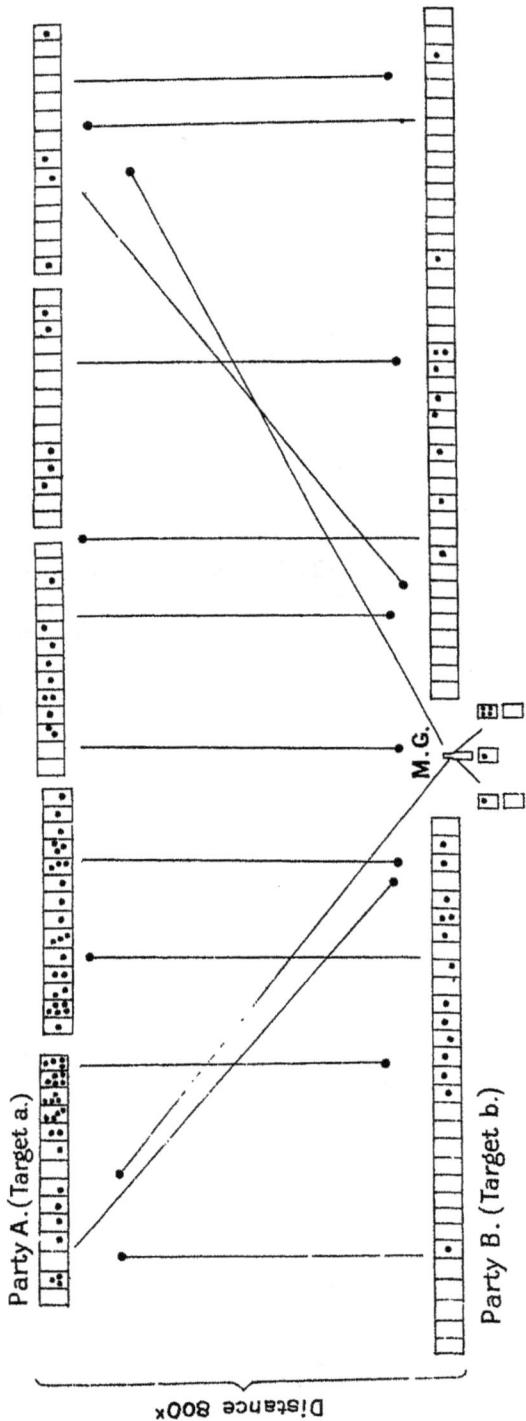

Party A. (Target a.)

Party B. (Target b.)

M.G.

Distance 800x

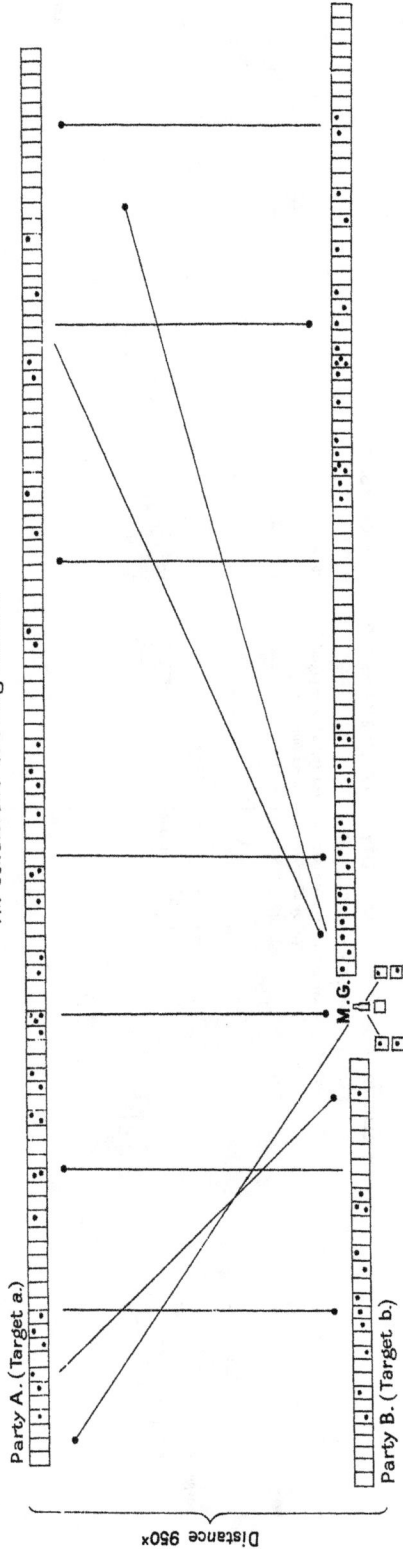

2. — AN ILLUSTRATION OF THE FACT THAT A FIRING LINE WITH A MACHINE GUN CAN BE SOMETIMES WORSTED BY A SIMILAR FIRING LINE WITHOUT ONE.

Combat between two equal infantry firing lines. One line (b) with a machine gun. The other line (a) without one. Lines in close order. All conditions of firing similar.

Party A. (Target a.)

M.G.

Party B. (Target b.)

Distance 950x

3.

AN ILLUSTRATION OF THE SUITABILITY OF MACHINE GUNS FOR RAPIDLY ENGAGING
FRESH TARGETS, AND CHANGING FROM ONE TARGET TO ANOTHER.

(a) & (b) are two exactly similar sets of targets; (a) is engaged by 35 riflemen,
(b) by 35 riflemen and a machine-gun.

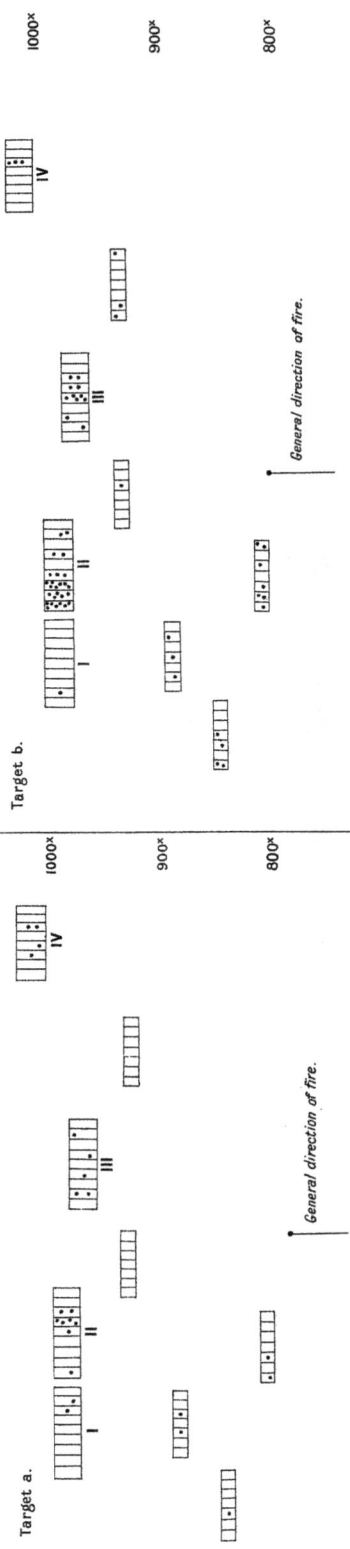

AN ILLUSTRATION SHOWING HOW FIRE EFFECT IS INFLUENCED BY POSTING MACHINE GUNS
(a) BEHIND THE INFANTRY FIRING LINE (b) IN THE INFANTRY FIRING LINE.

Conditions of firing the same in each instance

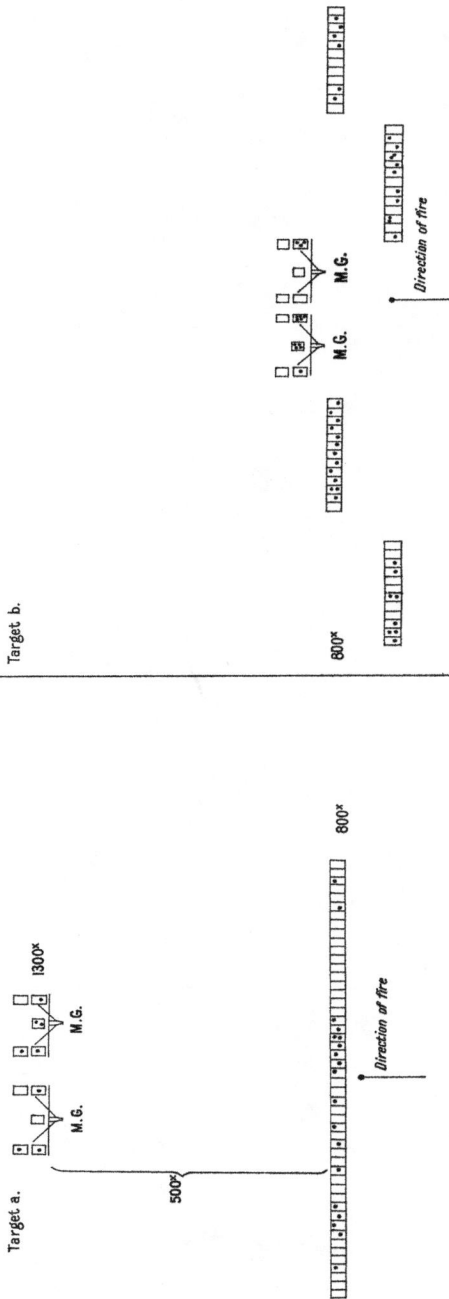